Knowing

Pat Mullan

Knowing

By Pat Mullan

ISBN-10:   0983865213
ISBN-13:   978-0983865216

An *ATHRY HOUSE* book

For *Cassidy* and *Sean Edward*, the newest
members of the Clan.

This is not a poetry collection.

Yes, there are poems here. And other writing too. I blog about *Clifden Arts Week* and I write down my thoughts as I walk around the streets of Galway on a dark day after a young lady dies in hospital. *Sicilian Odyssey* gives you some highlights of my visit to Sicily. In *'$48 dollars and a battered suitcase'* I get personal, letting you glimpse my youthful escapade as an Irish emigrant to Canada and the USA.

As I stated in the foreword to my last collection of poems, **Awakening**, I get most enjoyment from listening to a poet talk about the written work and the work in progress: *why a poem was written, the spark that ignited the vision, the snatch of overheard conversation, the incident that retrieves a past memory, the choice of words and imagery, the simple scene transformed, the need to be a witness.*

I don't think that any of my poems need an introduction. My work is simple, accessible, and unencumbered with intellectual reference; you won't need a degree in English literature to enable you to understand it. *Galway Kinnell*, whose Selected Poems won the 1983 Pulitzer Prize for poetry, takes issue with what he regards as two major misconceptions about poetry first, that it is unread and, second, that in order to be good, poetry should be unreadable: *"After the appearance of the great modernists, Eliot and Pound, when you really had to study poetry in graduate school to understand it, the audience for poetry was cut drastically, so when I started writing in the 50's, poetry did have a small, specialized following.   Since then there has been a dramatic change ... "*

Even though this is not a collection of poems, I hope that you find that everything here has a good, hard sense of poetry.

Pat Mullan,
Connemara, Ireland
April, 2013

"…the incident that retrieves a past memory….."

A Myriad of Knots

I watched you
Try to unravel knots in a cord
So you could tie up the meatloaf

Frustrated but philosophical,
You looked at me and said,
"A myriad of knots"
And I knew you meant
That life's complexity, and its mystery,
Was tied up in that ball of cord

Knotted to challenge us,
Knotted to engage us,
Knotted to impede us,
Knotted to teach us patience,
Knotted to teach us persistence,
Knotted to frustrate us,
Knotted to humble us

I watched you
Unravel those knots
Tie the meatloaf and walk away
Your brow unknotted for another day

Missing

There used to be a railroad here in this Connemara valley but it's missing. Its railbed is a relic of another age and I feel it has been returned to the *Great Gaels* who reigned over these hills. Maybe they are still here, if I could see clearly.

I would share these feelings with you if you were here. But you are missing today and all I have is the last text you sent to me: *I am in the art gallery looking at an exhibition of Francis Walker, Scottish artist. Wish you were with me. We could go 4 coffee.*

A cloud settles, like cotton wool, over the summit of Derryclare, and a double rainbow connects the Bens to the lough below, merging the past and the present, creating a parallel universe that only a few experience. I feel privileged and I wish you were here to share it with me.

Only poetry can say the things I feel now, only poets can interpret; the words of Carol Ann Duffy invade my mind: *all poems are love poems: missing words, missing things, missing people, missing love ...*

Blackout

I rode the New York subway that night just like every night.

My lifeline from Manhattan to the Bronx; oblivious of its clacks and clonks and its crush of human bodies, I trusted it to take me safely through. I watched my fellow passengers squeeze tighter together at every station, making room where there was none, hanging on to a space hard won, warily watching each new face that joined us as the doors slammed shut.

I rode the New York subway that night just like every night.

A squeamish stomach in the morning would never serve me well as I pushed into the garlic smell from those who'd eaten an alien meal, and I often guarded against an opportune feel. But in that very same milieu I learned a deeper lesson too, when a young man gave up a hard earned seat to get a lady off her feet, or when I'd observe the unlikely reader, one with hard worked hands, use chipped finger nails to turn the page.

I rode the New York subway that night just like every night.

At each new station the doors slid open to let some disembark and many others board and I'd watch the passing parade on the platform, strident, smart, sluggish, anxious, impatient, briefcases or bags, or nothing at all, newspaper clasped or open, or none at all, studiously avoiding each other, the body language of survival.

I rode the New York subway that night just like every night.

Sometimes the train would stop dead between stations without explanation and we'd wait in the stifling heat, silently suffering, sweating together, waiting patiently for a reprieve, always knowing that it would come, trusting that train to see us through before we succumbed to claustrophobia or lost our cool and blew it too; and then, that numbing feeling as we moved on, and the tunnel lights flashed by, hypnotizing us as we thundered through the ink-black tunnel.

I rode the New York subway that night just like every night.

Clutterbuck, Boughtflower, and Deadfield

A rose by any other name ...

But I found no comfort
In Shakespeare's words
That first Sunday morning
In the tailor's shop in Wembley

One day off the boat from Ireland
One day in a foreign land
Their London accent alien to me
My Ulster accent alien to them

Their names even more alien to my ear
Accustomed to the names at home:
O'Neill, McGuinness, Lynch, McHugh.
Clutterbuck, harsh and odd
Stuck to my tongue like glue

Boughtflower made me wonder
Why its owner never flinched
When asked to spell his name
He stood there proud as punch
His name his claim to fame

As the weeks passed, these names
Became familiar to my ear
Now fitting, with an exotic hue
They'd replaced those names of

Knowing   Pat Mullan

O'Neill, McGuinness, Lynch, McHugh

Until Mr Deadfield arrived one day
And turned my head around again
I couldn't say his name out loud
Because my brain screamed *cemetery*

But I discovered, as time passed,
That which Juliet knew: *Clutterbuck,*
Boughtflower, and Deadfield would,
were they not so called, retain
that dear perfection which they owe

And so I learned that Shakespeare was right:
What's in a name? That which we call a rose
By any other name would smell as sweet

Without Tears

-   *for Fr. Pat Mullan*

We bear the same name
And we share the same blood

But we took separate paths
On our journey through life

When young, you were an athlete
When old, you were a cripple

You look at me now, across the years,
Steadfast, strong, without any tears

I see you in your football gear,
A center forward, in '43 (was that the year)

And now I see you, in priestly gear,
Your ordination, a star for sure

Good looks, charisma, you had it all
You could have been on that silver screen

But you answered a different call
One to serve, that's where you stood

You never knew you'd be stricken down
By a deadly disease that would cripple you

You were only 25, a priest for a year or two,
When you were felled like a tree in the wood

Knowing   Pat Mullan

But the mettle inside stayed strong as steel
And you fought long and hard, to no avail

Your sentence confirmed, you dug deep inside
And healed others, I say this with pride

When I was in St. Columb's, you never knew
That I wouldn't follow the same path as you

You sent me a letter, £10 pounds inside
And I wanted to see you, sit by your side

So one day my father took me to Park
Your homestead, your haven, your ark

I knelt by your side, timorous and shy,
As you prayed over me, a glint in your eye

Your body infirm, your voice hoarse and dim,
I could still feel your strength radiate within

They said that the infirm come to your door
seeking a cure, they said that you cured the
incurable: that the diseased recovered and
the disabled walked again. They say that you
will be beatified, that you will become a saint.
But weren't you already a saint in this life?
You'd have been embarrassed by the many
who gathered for your funeral, by the media
coverage, by the fame.

Yes, we bear the same name
And we share the same blood

But that's where it begins and ends.

The Gist of It
- for Don Cunningham

"Give me the gist of it", he said,
"That's all I need"

"Give me a one-pager" he said.
And that's all he needed.

You might have been to Harvard B
Or even been to Wharton
And you thought your MBA
Made you superior in some way

But I'd watch you cringe
When he looked at you and said
"Just give me a one-pager"
And you knew that you were dead.

He taught me the bare essentials
And he did it with a grin
So don't quote Drucker to me
Because I was taught by him

"Give me the gist of it", he said.

Socks

"Socks make the man", she said.

"If you have a cow, you'll get a cow", she
said.

My mother's markers for life,
She's been gone seven years
And it cuts as sharp as a knife
But she left behind her wisdom
To help wash away the tears

She needed very few words
To convey the way she felt
She taught me how to tie my laces
And how to milk a cow
And how to fight my corner
To stand and never bow

"...the choice of words and imagery."

Hunkering Down

The quiet winter days are here
Dark and cold to bring
And we must hunker down
And wait it out till Spring

We could learn from the penguins
Who stand, their young at their feet,
And bravely face the Arctic winter
Each day without defeat

So it's time to hunker down
And use these days to contemplate
To live within the moment
And renew our inner state

The penguins all stand strong
In the very worst of weather
They teach us how to survive
Side by side, together

So dark and cold these days may be
But we will stand and fight
Those darker, gloomier thoughts
That would shut out all the light

The quiet winter days are here
Dark and cold to bring
And we must hunker down
And wait it out till Spring.

Spring

Spring is in the air
So why do I think of death
Spring is in the air
I can feel it on every breath

We walk up our Sunday hill, Connemara all
around; Bonny, our little white westie, leading
the way to higher ground. At the summit you
glide into *tai chi* transforming yourself, I can
see, while I sit on a flat boulder picking white
heather for you to wear

Spring is in the air
So why do I think of death
Spring is in the air
I can feel it on every breath

At the bridge we see an otter raise its head
from the placid peat-dark water and then duck
under, never to surface again. 'If I go before
you' I say 'my ashes blended with the water
below will carry my spirit forever'

Spring is in the air
So why do I think of death
Spring is in the air
I can feel it on every breath

Emerging

I've been a recluse for many days,
Locked up with my words and my muse
Engaged in combat with sentences
Paragraphs, chapters, clauses, and tenses

Winning one day, losing the next,
Lost in a forest of text
Searching for a path to follow
Paved with words that often seem hollow

And my muse would disappear
Leaving me lost, alone, and in fear
Words abandoned me at this time
I couldn't see, I knew I was blind

But my muse would always return
When my soul had started to burn
With words I'd stored for the fire
And we piled the pages higher and higher

With words that reached for the sky
And lifted me up there to fly
Where ordinary humans can not go
Only writers like Eugene Ionesco

Emerging into the sunlight once more
I stood uncertain at the front door,
Still haunted by chapters, clauses, and tenses
Making me doubt my own senses

Knowing

You're sitting behind me now

Knowing

That we are forever changing places
That sometimes you are behind me, and
Sometimes I am behind you, seeing
You rush ahead into our future, where
We stride together in lock-step,
A cadence born of a

Knowing

The Nude

Your *Nude*
Hangs, frameless, on my wall
Rescued from the attic
Days before a buried hoard
Of other work would disappear

Your *Still Life* hangs on another wall
And your *Celtic Art* of *Clonmacnoise*
hangs there boldly too
Our private gallery
dedicated to you

I imagine that the girl who sat for you
As relaxed as *Helga* in *Wyeth's Blue Velvet*
With burnished, almost drybrushed, hair
Would be proud to hang on my wall

Alabaster skin with a blush of shyness
Makes her glow, come alive before me
Almost demurely, she turns away
Velazquez would have put a mirror there
To show her face to me.

Floaters

I watched the young swallows float,
Giddily airborne in their new wings

Their parents sit still on the telephone wire
Watching them as they leave the nest

And today, floaters swim in the air
Before my eyes, like escaping swallows

And I wonder where you were
When I fled the nest

When I went too close to the fire,
When I flew higher and higher

Only to fall to earth
Far away from the nest

You were not there to watch me fly high
You were not there to watch me fall

And I look at these floaters before my eyes,
Wondering if they will fly away

Am I now an empty nest?
Am I sitting still, alone on the telephone wire?

Rooting

At midnight
I see you rooting
In our bedside wardrobe
For something astray
At the end of your day

And I see poetry imitating poetry
As Seamus Heaney's words invade,
"your head-down, tail-up hunt
in a bottom drawer for the black
plunge-line nightdress"

You come alive at midnight
Like some nocturnal animal
And I sink into sleep dreaming
Of your tail parading endlessly
Through your wardrobe
For something still astray.

"…the simple scene transformed."

Naked

The naked ribcage
Lies there to remind me that
This time is fleeting

Words inspired by the front cover of this book

To Talk of Many Things

"The time has come," the Walrus said, "To talk of many things:
Of shoes and ships and sealing-wax Of cabbages and kings
And why the sea is boiling hot And whether pigs have wings"
Lewis Carroll

I. Of fireside 'craic'

I must have been six years old. I watched them through the keyhole as they sat around the open hearth and listened to my Uncle Johnny tell tall tales of Port Moresby, Maracaibo, and his pet monkey, during his time in Africa, when it climbed into the tent rigging and peed down on the General Manager's dinner plate. And the McGuinness brothers, sitting by our fireside, smoking their white clay pipes (I'd dug many white clay pipes up from the ploughed earth, as though I was an archaeologist), and my mother with the large tea pot, filled as soon as it was emptied; I don't think it was ever empty from early morning till late at night.

II. Dream Sequence

I know I'm in Manhattan, but where? I walk and walk until I find myself in an unknown

neighborhood, is it uptown or downtown, is it
safe or dangerous? Suddenly two men walk
beside me, telling me not to step on the
flowers in the middle island - but there are no
flowers, only garbage and rubble in the
middle island. I cross to the street with no
people, only abandoned, burnt-out houses,
gaping windows, no panes, no frames - to find
the same two men following me, this time
riding bicycles, but I only see the face of one
of them: round, alien features, ginger
mustache and beard, and green, green eyes,
saying *"yeah, I grew up here" "yeah, they
don't like us now" "yeah, they don't like
green-eyed people"*

III. Of the Enslaved

The mind consumed, the heart, the brain, the
intellect saturated again, the image flickers,
the sound absorbs, and numbs the captured
silhouettes of ones once human, now enslaved
they wander aimlessly, disjointed, robot-like,
buffeted by forces not yet assigned to any
known dimension, controlled and not
controlled, free in their prison, imprisoned in
their freedom, congested in the subways of
New York and the tubes of London,
transported through the skies and beyond,
destination unknown, unmapped, searching,
always searching.

IV. And fish and more fish

The salmon of knowledge: salmon steaks, salmon darnes, smoked salmon, salmon-en-croute, salmon fettucini: Joe's Stone Crab in Miami, crab with mustard sauce; fish and chips (always chips in Ireland and Scotland, never French fries); the Chipper in Clifden, McDonagh's in Galway (some say it's the best fish in Ireland) but others say that Burdock's in Dublin is the best; Mr T's on Sanibel Island in Florida, Captain Norm's in the Hampton's; fish and chips in Moville, Donegal, wrapped in a newspaper and soaked in malt vinegar, herring fried in oatmeal in Craw, soused herring at Athry; skate, and silver darlings (herring) in Inverurie, kippers for breakfast in Thurso, salmon-en-croute at Athry, moules frites in France, mussels everywhere, the search for the best clam chowder, cockles dug from the beach in Connemara, Red Lobster in the US, sardines on toast, smoked mackerel, monkfish …

V. Of the Legacy

Festy's gone now, 'passed away like a gentle breeze', but we have his home-made walking sticks, wire puzzles, and *besoms* (brooms made from heather tied to a stick with tough twine, always carried in his pocket); these are his legacy to us, and I quote from my earlier poem to him: *'he's gone now, passed away like a gentle breeze, when the mist clings to*

the hills and silence seems to stop time, I
swear that I can still see him in the far
distance, jute bag over his shoulder, head at a
jaunty angle, leaning on his walking stick, his
voice carrying his memory back to me.'

VI. And the Garden

It's planting time in the garden: onions, sturon
or turbo; lettuce: Webb's wonderful or
iceberg; leeks: Musselburgh; parsley, triple
curled; turnips, early Milan or Snowball;
beetroot, Boltardy; peas, a dwarf variety such
as Kelvedon Wonder; potatoes: golden
wonders, Duke of York, Catriona. The ground
must be all dug over and raked smooth before
starting   a long plank or planks are handy for
walking on to avoid tramping on the ground
which should be dry on top before planting
plant onions in rows, about one foot apart,
individual sets about four inches apart   push
into soft ground so that they are just beneath
the surface of the earth and not showing at all
otherwise the birds tend to pull them out
detach any long, one or two inch, wispy parts
of the original shoot before planting

VII. Of the Millennium

You said we should bury something deep in
the ground to tell them we'd been here or
plant a tree that will live and grow, to stand

tall like a redwood when we are gone but what would we bury: old photos, letters, DVDs, the Sunday papers. Isn't it presumptuous to think that we have something worthy of leaving behind and when do you suggest that our 'time capsule' be opened: in a hundred years, five hundred years, maybe the next millennium   but this is the next millennium; and what did 'they' bury in the ground for us; is there something buried in Queen Maeve's tomb waiting there for us; was the Tollund man buried for us to find; did they find Ogham written on the walls of the stone cellars in the New World; was that left for us; did Columbus come to Galway to get directions to the New World: a memorial stone in Galway's Spanish parade, claims that "On these shores, around the year 1477, the Genoese sailor Cristoforo Colombo found sure signs of land beyond the Atlantic. La Città di Genova alla Città di Galway. 29.VI.1992 ; will another Columbus, in the next millennium, go to Houston to find directions to help him discover new planets ...

Groatie Buckies

April first, it's your birthday today,
And you laugh at that, deep in your throat,
As we walk on the beach at Dog's Bay,
Galway's western shore, sensing the magic
Of this place, where the plate-glass sheen
Of the sea meets creamy soft sand, and
Rock-pocked hills comfort the soul.

Where would we be if not here, I thought?
Miami, New York, London, Paris, Chicago?
No! We traded their bright city lights for
These starry starry skies of Connemara.

Bonny, our little white furry-coated westie
Runs ahead, chasing seaweed flotsam,
Tail wagging, tongue lapping the purest of air
From the Atlantic Ocean, the same air,
I could imagine, that had crossed
The beaches of Cohasset, only hours ago.

We climbed the primrose-painted hill and
Followed Bonny as she ran to the Atlantic,
Disappearing, reappearing in the undulating
Green, dipping into one micro-climate after
Another, one bathed in warm sunshine,
Another shadowed above, spongy underfoot,
Carpeted (it seemed) to challenge us to feel,
To see, and we did, our senses heightened.

We stopped and stood beside a huge Celtic

Knowing   Pat Mullan

Standing stone, one planted by nature herself,
And we planted our wish-stones on top,
Two small rocks to testify for us.
I don't know yours and you don't know mine
Yet I'm sure our wishes know each other.

Back on the beach , we trace the necklace
Of seaweed and the trail of seashells, guiding
Us out of Dog's Bay, tempting us to stay.
I stooped down to pick up a shell,
Coloured like a butterfly's wings, while
You searched for Groatie Buckies,
Those cowries of good luck, capturing
A childhood spent with your dad, watching
His eyes scan the sand for Groatie Buckies.

You found five Groatie Buckies,
I found none, but I left Dog's Bay happy,
Knowing that I shared your win.

Sean Halpenny, *bodhrán* player

The first time I saw you play
My soul flipped over that day
Watching the *bodhrán* and the man
Transformed into a one-man band.

You started drumming gently
Until you had me hypnotized
And then you played intently
Until you had me mesmerized

It seemed to me that you had merged
And the *bodhrán* and you were one
As though an alchemist had forged
A living instrument to stun

The drum and you lost focus
And your hands became a blur
And I'm sure I left my body then
And in that pub, nothing stirred

I've often seen you play since then
And the magic has not died
So I know your DNA's in that *bodhrán*
It's your body and blood, your pride.

The bodhrán (plural *bodhráns* or *bodhráin*)
is an Irish frame drum ranging from 25 to 65 cm (10" to 26") in
diameter, with most drums measuring 35 to 45 cm (14" to 18").
The sides of the drum are 9 to 20 cm (3½" to 8") deep.
A goatskin head is tacked to one side (synthetic heads, or other
animal skins are sometimes used). The other side is open ended
for one hand to be placed against the inside of the drum head to
control the pitch and timbre.

Coole

I listened to the silence
on the shores of Turlough
The busy whispering of birds
Carrying the soothing sounds
of *'peace dropping slow, filled
with the linnets' wings'*

And, in the mid-distance, the
shoreline melted into soft grey,
a narrow blanket at the start of day.

I'd never been to Coole before,
and I was afraid that it might
not live up to my expectations,
that that imagined world of Yeats
and Lady Gregory would disappoint.

At the water's edge, a lady sat, her
eyes sparkling in the sun, writing
in a small notebook, and I wondered:
What is she writing ? Poems, private thoughts,
maybe a love letter to Yeats.

I expected to see the wild swans,
W.B. promised them to me, didn't he?
Did they leave when he left ?
Somehow I felt bereft.

But the trees of Coole rescued me:
I read their names on the signs that
told me the scouts had been there

Knowing   Pat Mullan

to help them reproduce, and then I knew
that those trees were carrying Yeats
and Lady Gregory into our future

Coole did not disappoint me,
my imagined world still thrives.

Always

Ben Lettery, crowned by a rainbow
And clothed in a gossamer mist
Lifted me out of this valley
Transporting me to other places,
Other times

You're always somewhere else, she said
Calling me back to the present
I answered (as I usually did):
I'm writing in my head

The mist, now settled in the valley,
Masked the Bens and the lough
And I was off again elsewhere
Until I heard her cough

Moving close, I startled her
Sorry, I was thinking, she said
Realizing that she too had been
Somewhere else

Prince Edward Island

Your roads end in unpaved red soil
Your beach at Canning turns to mud

And I wonder: am I in the New World
Or suspended in some purgatory

In Pictou you show us your ship Hector
And I learn the story of your founding Scots

Evicted by the Duke of Sutherland to cling
In misery at Bad Bea, that barren, rocky

Infertile ground where only the hardiest
Might survive, and transported from Scotland

To promised prosperity in this New World
Where he dumped you from his ship, the Polly

In the dead of winter, to chop down trees
To build shelter from the elements

I stand here at Orwell Corners, knowing you'd
Survived, the farms ring out your names:

Gillis, Murchison …and I watch Barry Gillis
Toss the caber at your Highland Games

And I listen to Chester Gillis explain how he
made the man on a 'perpetual motion' ladder

Your farms are prosperous, your land is rich
You have survived, you will survive

Fire on the hill

It simmered, spluttered, fizzled out
Then reignited, flamed again
We stood, captured in its throes
Did Hell spring to mind just then?

Sated by *moules marinières avec frites*
And a very good red Bordeau
We'd been 'blessed' by the Cross
At the last crossroads we saw

The workers had lit a barbecue
And let the fire spill over
Knowing that the hills were safe
We watched the flames faint flicker

But the sun had set and yet
It still seemed bright outside
The fire had spread, the hill alight
Tall trees flamed like candles

The pyre grew higher and higher
The flames climbed and climbed
The fire had spread, the hills on fire
Could this be Hell this time?

My Poetry Shelf

Why does poetry talk to me now
In ways that failed me before
Why does it finally allow me
To enter its long-shut door

The poetry books on my shelves
Have been unopened, unread
Since I placed them there
In homage to the word

Cellared like very good wine
They've matured on these shelves of mine
Waiting to be decanted
Finally to be wanted

So I'll go from shelf to shelf
In no particular order
Because I believe that poetry itself
Breaks down every border

If I name names
This will become another list
And if I read to you
You'll tell me to desist

So I'll go from shelf to shelf
Of poems both old and new
And here and there I'll choose a book
To share today with you

But the morning news has just arrived to tell me that Ray Bradbury has died, stopping me cold in my tracks and sending me on a hunt through the racks till I find his *New and Selected Poems:I Live by the Invisible* And I open at the very first poem, how appropriate:

Let me read to you:

To Ireland.

I dare not go – that isle has ghosts
And spectral rains along the coasts
Such rains as weep their loss in tears
Till I am drowned in sunken years.
When last I walked a Dublin street,
My gaze was clear, my pulses fleet,
Now half a life or more is gone
I cannot face sad Dublin's dawn.

But I must move on to Irish poets, some now gone and others who never sought fame but have become a household name: W.B. Yeats, Seamus Heaney, Paul Muldoon, Paul Durcan, Michael Longley, Eamon Grennan, Tony Curtis, Michael Coady, Anthony Cronin, Mary O'Malley, Tom Paulin, Oscar Wilde, Louis MacNeice, Brian Merriman, John Montague, Patrick Kavanagh, Padraic Colum, Joan McBreen, Gerard Hanberry, James Simmons, Gerald Dawe, Medbh McGuckian, Thomas Kinsella, Derek Mahon …

But I must stop, it goes on and on
I said I wouldn't make a list,
I lied, I lied, how could I resist

So I'll apologize for those I've missed

And I'll apologize to Yeats for stealing from him:

On The Way To Connemara

A funny thing happened on the way to Connemara when I met the young lady on the Costa Golf Course in the designer jogging suit with her ears wrapped in a Sony Walkman, her right hand pumping the phallic steel of the latest fad while her left hand fed her Jane Fonda body thousands of units of stress vitamins from a naturally clear intravenous like straw that parted her Aspen toned lips and connected with a non-biodegradable container emblazoned in the pastel blues and pinks of Florida ... I will arise and go now and go to Connemara where time goes dropping slow and live where the air is filled with linnets wings and poteen stills abound in the bee loud glades

We'll return to the shelves and dive back in, sifting through in stops and starts, until we find the Russians. Yevtushenko stands apart, a rebel voice true to heart, who says that *'art's eternal role is the uniting of human hearts in the name of goodness and justice'*

Now the Scottish poets want a voice and I tell them it's not my choice to forget Robert Louis Stevenson, Hugh MacDiarmid or Douglas Dunn and if I left out Sorley MacLean then I'd not be welcome in Scotland again but

Knowing   Pat Mullan

Robert Burns says it all: *'a man's a man for a that'*

The English poets are all there, hoarded from my boarding school where I was punished without care and Wordsworth, Chesterton, Browning, Tennyson, Masefield, Shelly, and Keats were names that threatened to defeat

But I stole their words and hid them well:

Tiger, tiger, burning bright
In the forests of the night ...

I will go down to the sea in ships,
In tall ships ....

Said the walrus to the carpenter
To speak of many things
Of sealing wax and sailing ships and cabbages and kings

The Great Gaels of Ireland are the men that God made mad,
For all their wars are merry and all their songs are sad

But Philip Larkin, Roger McGough and Carol Ann Duffy have rescued them.

A whole shelf of American poets stare boldly down at me today and I can hear Walt Whitman say: *'The United States themselves are essentially the greatest poem. The English language befriends the grand American expression ... it is brawny enough, and limber and full enough'* And Maya Angelou says firmly: *'I shall not be moved'* And Ginsberg needs only one word: *'Howl'* I read their names from left to right and try as hard as I might I promised not to make a list but you'd never forgive me if I missed to name each name on sight: Robert Frost, Carl Sandburg, Robert Lowell, Richard Wilbur, Louise Glick, T. S. Elliott, Emily Dickinson, Henry David Thoreau, Henry Wadsworth Longfellow, Anne Sexton, Ralph Waldo Emerson, Edgar Allan Poe, W. S. Merwin, Theodore Roethke, Galway Kinnell, Dan Masterson,

And James Dickey, of whom I wrote the following:

James Dickey's Poetry:
The Religious Dimension

But let me say that I have always been against traditional religion because my religion has been so personal to me. I always felt that God and I have a very good understanding, and the more the ritualistic services go on, the more God and I stand by and laugh. I don't believe that the God that created the universe has any interest in the dreadful kind of self-abasement men go through in religious ceremonies.

Those are the words of James Dickey. This personal religion of Dickey's is Christian, paganistic, Hindu-like, and primitive: a cauldron of supernatural potions that creates in the poet his need to blend man and beast, natural and supernatural, reality and fantasy, into a recipe that leaves him with a fear of death (not physical death, but mortality), a search for a reincarnate continuity of existence and a need to define the state of afterlife.

And E. M. Schorb, an Award winning American poet who should be more widely known, and about whose work, *Manhattan Spleen*, I wrote: *Manhattan Spleen* is a rich and complex smorgasbord of 57 prose poems; sustenance for mind, body and soul. In the title of this engrossing work, E.M Schorb tips his hat to Charles Baudelaire (*Paris Spleen*), the nineteenth century French poet that we credit with giving birth to the prose poem. Yet this is truly an American work, as American as Walt Whitman. One might say that Whitman's lines describe Schorb's work: *A vast similitude interlocks all, All spheres, grown, ungrown, small, large, suns, moons, planets   All distances of place however wide, All distances of time, all inanimate forms, All souls, all living bodies.* Each poem in *Manhattan Spleen* probes the depth of our understanding, explores the porous barrier between our real and imagined worlds, asks us to delve beneath the surface and question the truths that we have taken for granted.

Buried deep between Eamon Grennan's *Wildly For Days* and Herman Hesse's *Poems*, a book on *haiku* peeks out, a gift from my Japanese friend, Mana, and I pick it up to read from *Somokuto* by Taneda Santoka, who became a Zen monk at the age of 43 and

Knowing   Pat Mullan

travelled all over Japan as a mendicant monk;
these *haiku* are markers on his journey:

Sprawling for a rest,
On my legs still –
Sunlight.

Stretching ahead –
The straight road,
Loneliness.

It's drizzling,
Here I am,
Still alive.

In the water,
A traveller's reflection –
As I pass.

Me –
Helpless and good for nothing,
Walking.

You gave me this present, Mana, this book on
haiku and I knew what you meant, without
knowing your language – and I wrote in *haiku*
for you:

The little brown bird
Dies on this bright May morning
Hitting the window

Looking back at the
Sun setting over the hill
I am walking tall

Knowing   Pat Mullan

We shared this May day
Of high skies over Corrib
And picked wild flowers

I am a strange woman; I am a free spirit, you
said, and, at midnight, you wrote a poem for
me;

You know the colour of the sky in English
I know the smell of the flowers in Japanese
And we know the image of everything
Don't need anything

And then you were gone.

"… the need to be a witness."

I love the smell of toasted bagels in the morning ...

There's a sheen of early rain on the streets of Galway as I walk towards Eyre Square. Some people walk, heads covered, against the showers; others walk, heads uncovered, seeming to relish the rain on their faces, impervious to the cold.

I pass the Bagel Factory and I can't resist. I need my morning coffee, my American addiction, and I love the smell of toasted bagels in the morning. A large americano, a plain toasted bagel, cream cheese on the side, the daily newspaper borrowed from the shelf, and all is right with the world.

But the newspaper headlines destroy my appetite: outrage and sadness as 1,000 attend a vigil in a woman's memory. A young woman had died from septicemia in the hospital because her foetus still had a heartbeat and, even though it stood no chance of survival, they refused to abort it. The darkness has set over Galway this morning, set over our bright, joyous, upbeat, modern western city, city of culture, university city, city of The Tribes. My bagel is cold and has lost its smell, my coffee is tepid and sits, forgotten, in front of me.

Knowing   Pat Mullan

I am angry. I walk away from my coffee and bagel. I walk out on to the street, now drying under the emerging sun. People are smiling, as usual. Cheerful faces, lights that lift the spirit and change a walk to a float. But not today. I am angry. Angry at the loss of a beautiful young Indian woman. Angry at the darkness, angry at the failure to make laws which protect. I look around and see a city filled with people from all cultures, all religions, all ethnic backgrounds. I hear Polish voices, Russian voices, German voices, French voices, English voices, American voices. I see African faces, Asian faces, Oriental faces, Indian faces, fair-skinned and dark-skinned Irish faces. And I think: Ireland is changing but its laws are not. Its soul is still a captive of the religion of its past. I know that that will change, I have to believe that, I would not have returned if I hadn't. And I let my anger subside.

I wander down Shop Street, bustling with people, noisy, talkative, the closest atmosphere to Boston or New York. Young and old, male and female, black and white, straight and gay, mobile phones embedded in ears, communicating here, there, everywhere: a nation of talkers gone global; our stories, our history was always oral, eons passed before we wrote anything down, it's no wonder that mobile phones and ebooks suit us so well: we are oral again! No waiting now until the world finds out what we have to say.

Knowing   Pat Mullan

I pass Lynch's Castle, now a bank, and I try to
imagine what life was like in the days when
the Tribes ran Galway, the fourteen merchant
families who dominated the political,
commercial, and social life of the city of
Galway between the 13th and 16th centuries
and, in my head, I write their names: Athy,
Blake, Bodkin, Browne, D'Arcy, Deane, Font,
French, Joyce, Kirwan, Lynch, Martyn,
Morris, Skerrett.

I stop at the window of Dubray Books and
wave to Matthew who tells me, with some
trepidation, that he is retiring soon. I hesitate
and then move on, fighting my addiction,
knowing that, if I went in, I'd be there far too
long – just like I used to when I entered
Kenny's before they closed, a bookstore
designed to entrap; now they have gone into
cyberspace and it's not the same at
http://www.bookshop.kennys.ie/ so I walk on,
dodging the people, mentally filing their faces
and attitudes, knowing that this is my milieu,
my drug, my sustenance.

The smell of fish and chips wafts under my
nose as I pass McDonagh's and I know I'll be
back, but the magnetic pull of the Corrib river
drags me on, and I stand on the bridge
watching the water rush out into Galway Bay.
I watch the swans glide towards me, white
galleons I imagine, and I turn and walk
towards Spanish Arch where galleons from
Spain once sailed up Galway Bay with
cargoes of wine...

'And catch the heart off guard and blow it open'

...at the Clifden Arts Week

I live in Connemara now in a place called Recess where smart alecs recently added an 'ion' to the road sign turning it into Recession, fitting I suppose for the time that is in it – as they say in the Irish syntax; and now syntax becomes sin-tax in my head and I wander off somewhere, wondering if all our sins were taxed would the recession end overnight ...

Sub-prime loans, Madoff, global warming, 9/11, Al-Qaeda, healthcare, swine flu, the Real IRA, taxes, emigration, immigration, illegal aliens, the God delusion, paedophile priests, Iraq, Iran, Afghanistan, Palestine, the West Bank, Israel, Gaza Strip, outstrip, Hamas, PLO, ETA, cars, pollution, General Motors, Anglo-Irish Bank, too big to fail, bankruptcy, suicides, jail, crisis, depression, recession, bears, bulls, bullies, bears, bares all, airport bombs, train bombs, nightclub bombs, suicide bombers, nuclear bombs, dirty bombs, dirty language, pornography, internet porn, inflation, deflation, derivatives, contracts for difference...

*No, no, no, I've come to Arts Week in Clifden
to dispel all that gloom; this annual week of
magic and treasure, treasure free of global
speculation, treasure that has only increased
in value over time ...*

Seamus Heaney needed no introduction when
he came to read at St. Joseph's Church
but *Des Lally* outdid himself; and the church
was filled to the rafters with people of all
ages, young and old, Irish people, Connemara
people, people from other countries,
academics, farmers, fishermen, bus drivers,
teachers, builders, labourers, mothers,
teenagers, students, poetry readers, people
who never read poetry, people who had never
seen a Nobel Prize winner before, fans, poetry
slammers, groupies there to see *'famous
Seamus'* ...and then he started to read: old
poems, new poems, famous poems, heart-
rending poems: *'a four foot box, a foot for
every year'* , heart-opening poems: *'and catch
the heart off guard and blow it open'* ...

In the Station House Theatre, as I waited
for *Paul Muldoon*, the man sitting beside me
said, in awe, *"you know he's the poetry editor
of The New Yorker now"* and, no, I didn't
know that, I only knew that he lectured at
Princeton and that he'd won the Pulitzer Prize
for *Moy Sand and Gravel* (a sand pit has never
looked the same to me since then) and I
remembered that he'd signed his poems to me

all those years ago in London after his reading
at the Royal Court Theatre where we'd sat
beside *Brian Cox* (who has since fled to
Hollywood) … but I digress, *Paul* will make
you do that, read him and you'll see what I
mean … and suddenly he was there, same
face, same hair, a little greyer now, same
Ulster voice tinged now with a bit of America
… and the time flew by just listening to him
until he asked us if we had twenty-five (or
was it thirty-five) minutes to give him so that
he could read *Incantata* … who would say no
… and we listened, spellbound, to Paul read
the work that he wrote to the memory of his
former lover, Mary Powers, who died from
cancer… *Incantata* is a long magical elegy of
forty-five eight line stanzas that opens with
these lines: *I thought of you tonight, a leanbh,*
lying there in your long barrow colder and
dumber than a fish by Francisco deHerrera …

And everywhere: *Tony Curtis*, poet-in-
residence, with his charisma, his captivating
poetry, the twinkle in his eyes, welcomed to a
reading in the Clifden Library by *Paul* and
Bernie, librarians and custodians of our
treasures; reading to a star-struck audience, all
listening, listening, knowing that his poems
would never sound the same when they read
them, wondering if he was born a poet and,
knowing, at the end, that he truly was … to be
followed, matched, book-ended by *Michael*
Coady, poet-in-residence before *Tony*, who
took us through his hypnotizing recent work,
set mostly in Paris.

People squeezed into the Church of Ireland's pews as they listened to *Cantairi Chonamara* commence the evening with *Vivaldi's Gloria* – an opening to pepare the audience for *Anuna*. If music 'soothes the savage breast' then *Anuna* must deserve the award for the most soothing of them all, the men holding us from the moment they moved up the aisle, stopping midway and singing to us, transfixing us, letting us breathe again as they reached the altar, only to immediately submerge us in the dramatic entrance of the *Anuna* ladies, gowned in medieval attire, beautiful in face and voice, each holding a candle as they moved up the aisles, centre and side, covering us with their presence, their poise, their perfection, their voices, soothing, soothing, soothing …

At the Atlantic Hotel I fell headlong into the visual arts; the work of the artist *Alannah Robins*. Her work insisted that I explore the walls of the hotel, its exposition space, until I arrived back again at her triptych which dominated the exhibition: the shipwrecked *Plassey*, haunting and proud, breaking up now on the Inis Oirr island rocks, captured in three parts; easily a masterpiece commanding all of us to pay homage to those who 'go down to the sea in ships' and to *Alannah Robins*, the artist, a lady of many talents who had enthralled us earlier as mezzo-soprano in her classical music recital in the Church of

Ireland, accompanied by *Sister Karol O'Connell* of *Kylemore Abbey* on the piano, as they presented pieces by Schubert, Mozart, Field and Poulenc…

And what can one say of *Eamon Grennan*, poet, lecturer at Vassar, NYU, Columbia; a man whose home is here and there: New York for half the year, Connemara for the other half. Former US poet laureate *Billy Collins* said: *'Few poets are as generous as Eamon in the sheer volume of delight his poems convey.'* *Eamon* held us in the Clifden Library with his readings; now he holds us at home as we savour his book, *Out of Breath*, saying to ourselves 'why haven't we read him before, he's so good …'and earlier he had surpassed himself in a dramatic recital for two voices, which he had adapted from *J.M.Synge's The Aran Islands.*

Acted and delivered by *Tegolin Knowland and Sean Coyne*, it was an enthralling performance bringing *Synge* and the people of the Aran Islands to life in front of us; a performance that, had it been given on Broadway, would surely have captured a Tony Award …

How do I cover poet *Michael Longley*, appointed Professor of Poetry for Ireland in 2007, and guitarist *Redmond O'Toole*, selected as the National Concert Hall's 'rising star' for 2009. An event of poetry and music, extraordinary. *Michael's* poem, Ceasefire, hangs on the wall in my house and I was stunned by *Redmond** at last year's Arts Festival in the more intimate space of the Clifden Library. This time *Michael* and *Redmond* are in a much grander setting, the stage at the Station House Theatre. But they still made us feel intimate, made us feel that they were right there in our living room. Alternating *Michael's* poemswith *Redmond's* music catered to our emotional centre, at once opening us to a unique poetic vision complemented by innovative and exciting music. Michael celebrated his 70th birthday and *Brendan Flynn* (founder of the Clifden Arts Week) congratulated him as artist *Rosie McGurran* presented him with a portrait...

*Redmond *has emerged as one of the most innovative and exciting young guitarists in Europe; the first to adapt to Paul Galbraith's new groundbreaking technique and instrument; he plays an 8-string 'Brahms guitar' in the cello position connected to a special resonating box. The additional range of the guitar allows an expansion of the repertoire as well as incorporating original music for classical guitar.*

And the Clifden Arts Week would not be complete without one or more classical concerts, many of them held in the Church of Ireland. And so it was there that I went to listen to ... and watch ... *Finghin Collins*, one of Ireland's most superb pianists, a student of the Geneva Conservatoire and sought after internationally...andcellist/conductor/compos er *Christian Benda*, Chief Conductor and

Artistic Director of the Prague Sinfonia (and a descendant of the *Czech Benda* composers dynasty of the 18th century) … yes, listen and watch them (because it was as much a visual experience as an aural) play Schumann, Shostakovich, and Brahms …

Speaking of a visual experience, we had a real treat: the first screening in Ireland of *Art O'Briain's* new documentary film, *A Subtle Movement of Air*, presented by *Art* himself. The film is a moving portrait of *Evald Grog,* a Dane who has suffered from Muscular Dystrophy all his life, a disease he has not allowed to prevent him from overcoming the challenges and impediments caused by his condition. It follows him in his personal journey from the simple act of getting bathed to the massive achievement of his pioneering work in establishing support centres in Denmark for people like himself … and now farther afield in Iceland where he has gone to consult, show, exhort all who encounter him, from ordinary Icelanders to government ministers … to get them to follow the example of Denmark. Truly a tribute to *Evald Grog* – and to the skill and dedication of *Art O'Briain* in bringing *Evald* to us. This is a film deserving world-wide distribution. It is inspiring and uplifting.

Obama gets the Nobel Peace Prize, green shoots are spotted in the economy, the stock markets may have hit a bottom, the Americans and the Iranians are talking, the US will not build missile bases on Russia's border, Guantanamo will be closed, Obama bans torture, more green shoots are seen, Madoff goes to prison, there's some light at the end of the tunnel, the Celtic Tiger is dead, long live the Celtic Tiger, windmills, solar panels, green energy, recycling, bank regulation, slow recovery seen on the horizon, depression avoided ...

It seems that the gloom in the world is lifting and some sunshine is peeking through the clouds ... could any of that be attributed to the Clifden Arts Week ... no, no, no, highly improbable ... and yet ...

KOREA

Land of the Morning Calm
The Ireland of Asia

UIJONGBU

He stared at us:
Intruders.
His face, weather-worn:
Inscrutable.

We trudged, single-file:
Uncaring.
We looked, right through:
Incurious.

His feet in muddy water:
Correct.
Toil-worn pants rolled to knees:
Timeless.

Our olive-greens, dusty:
Foreign.
Rifles shoulder-slung, empty:
Protectors.

His eyes, small, (seemed) sad:
Resentment.
Bare arms, sinewy, blend:
Belong.

We pass, uninvited:
Untouched.
He stoops, unbending:
Ageless.

The Bridge of No Return

Panmunjom
    Panmunjom
        Panmunjom

Repeat it often
Soft and gentle
Feel it slide over your teeth
Its silken breeze across your tongue

Panmunjom
    Panmunjom

It sings to me of truces
Of swords rusting in rice paddies
Of hope, of peace, of time to heal

Panmunjom

My destination on that Thanksgiving day. Did
I go to give thanks, did I expect turkey, maybe
stuffing too. What would the Pilgrims have
thought; would they have expected a
Thanksgiving table, did they expect that from
the Indians. Did I expect to be greeted by
North Koreans and South Koreans. No, I did
not. I wished for these things. I wished for an

end to the DMZ, an end to a divided country, an end to a divided world, peace at last …and I think now that, had John Lennon been there, he would surely have said, *"Imagine there's no countries, it isn't hard to do, nothing to kill or die for, imagine all the people living in peace, you may say I'm a dreamer, but I'm not the only one, I hope some day you'll join us and the world will be as one*

Imagine!   I imagined that I heard singing in my head, that I heard a chorus of:

Panmunjom
    Panmunjom
        Panmunjom

Say it in your head, say it again and again, Say it with passion, say it in celebration, Say it, say it, say it …

And then I woke up on that bus, woke up to the Freedom Road, woke up to the barbed wire, the observation posts, the machine gun emplacements in the hills. I woke up to the cold reality, a feeling of trepidation, even fear. No sign of Thanksgiving, no welcoming committee, no one to greet us, only North Korean soldiers in large greatcoats, making them taller and wider, giving them a threatening presence.

Panmunjom

I whispered it now,
Silently in my head,
Spoke it like a vow,
To protect me ahead.

Ushered into the Joint Security Area, I entered the blue, one-story building where the North Koreans and the Chinese meet the South Koreans and the Americans of the United Nations Command.   Here they sit at the conference table, green velvet placed directly over the border line which bisects the table. Flags of the Northern side stand on small wooden flag poles at the North Korean end, and flags of the Southern side stand on similar small wooden flag poles at the South Korean end. I knelt down to observe the table top at eye level and I am sure that the Northern flag poles were marginally taller than the Southern ones. It also seemed to me that the seats of their conference chairs were marginally higher. A calculated psychological advantage. Maybe. Or were my eyes playing tricks on me. Outside doves fly in the air but only seem to land on the roofs of the North Korean huts, never on the roofs of the South Korean huts. Have these doves of peace chosen the true peacemakers. As I have said, maybe my eyes were playing tricks on me.

Knowing   Pat Mullan

Panmunjom

Outside an eerie silence obtains
Soldiers from the North stand guard
Soldiers from the South stand guard
A stand-off from which no one gains

Dusk is settling over it all and soon it will be time to leave. But first I stood looking out over *the bridge of no return,* the bridge into North Korea. In the far distance a cluster of lights brighten the skyline, seeming to illuminate a village, a town, a settlement. Laughter and music carry through the evening air, sounds of happiness and joy. Were my ears playing tricks on me? Did I imagine this too? Or was this their trick, one to flaunt their good life?

I have never returned but it haunts me still.

Panmunjom
    Panmunjom
        Panmunjom

Say it in your head, say it again and again,
Say it with passion, say it in desperation,
Say it, say it, say it …

And today the airwaves resound with threats:
An unnamed spokesman in Pyongyang's
Foreign Ministry office said North Korea will
launch *"a preemptive nuclear attack to
destroy the strongholds of the aggressors"*

As I write this, the U.N. Security
Council, comprised of six world powers (the
United States, France, Britain, Germany,
China and Russia), is set to vote on a new
round of sanctions against North Korea,
following their third nuclear test.

Panmunjom

It haunts me still.

SICILY

*"let me take you to Sicily, to the
Sicily of the senses, the place of
wine and roses, of antipasta, modica
chocolate, and marsala wine".*

Sicilian Odyssey

John Ashbery says,

"To be a writer and write things you must have experiences you can write about. Just living won't do."

I have been to Sicily and that is the experience I want to write about, just living those days there won't do. So let me take you to Sicily, to the Sicily of the senses, the place of wine and roses, of antipasta, modica chocolate, and marsala wine. But first I must take you to the Sicily of the soul, the place of Greek amphitheatre, Roman catacombs, Norman Cathedrals, and Arab roots, a place where the ancient world met and fought, a place that inspired poets, artists, visionaries. This is not a work of poetry. It is a tribute to Sicily. Many poems lie hidden here. Over time they will appear.

I will only take you to the places and experiences that stay close to my heart. Otherwise this would become a tourist travelogue.

Palermo

We are captured by the center, the *"Quattro Canti" (Four Corners)* where *Corso Vittorio Emanuele* crosses *Via Maqueda,* and Spanish Kings and Patron saints look down from their doric columns. Then we go to the *Palazzo Del Normani* to see the ceiling of the *Capella Palatino*, the private royal chapel of the Norman King Roger II

Next morning, *La Nuciria*, the market where fishmongers call out and fruit and vegetables make the mouth water, we gaze at stalls of bric-a-bracin a maze of streets. and eat ice cream in the *Piazza S. Domenica*

Next stop is the *Giardino Garibaldi.* A nearby building is connected to *Giuseppe Tomasi di Lampedusa (1896-1957), Duke of Palma,* and *Prince of Lampedusa, who wrote Il Gattopardo (The Leopard).*

Duomo di Monreale

The bus from *Porto Nuevo* to *Monreale,* takes us to *Il Duomo*, perched on a mountaintop overlooking *Palermo.* We enter, our eyes drawn heavenwards to 42 huge golden glowing Byzantine mosaics of Old Testament and New Testament scenes and the golden mosaics that frame the altar hypnotize us into a loss of time and place. Built of golden Sicilian stone by *King William II* the *Duomo* combines Moorish and Norman styles and is famed for its multicolored mosaics.A huge, majestic *Christ the Pantocrator* broods over it all in the central apse.

The church was adorned with flowers and ribbons, in readiness for a wedding. Suddenly the organ strikes up and the beautiful bride is led down the aisle by her proud father, with an adoring flower girl looking on – a magical moment !

On our last night in *Palermo*, we end it among the 'beautiful people', sitting outside the *Hotel Paradiso*, drinking margaritas and beer, entertained by a young black man with a mobile disco unit.

From Ponte di Naso, Sinagra, Ucria to Taormina

We decide to take the 'scenic route' to *Taormina* - somewhere between *Palermo* and *Messina* we leave the motorway and head for the hills. Climbing higher and higher over twisting, winding roads, sheer drops below, we pass through the small villages of *Ponte di Naso, Sinagra, Ucria*. It's a white-knuckle drive.

At the summit, fog descends and it starts to rain. As we twist our way down we don't see the precipices that we teeter above.

Finally we drive across a viaduct through mid-air into Taormina.

Taormina

We enjoy a superb dinner in the very jolly *Al Giardino* restaurant which specializes in seafood and pasta, and is situated across the street from *Taormina's* unique botanical garden, a must visit for next day.

And next day that's what we did, crossed the street into the botanical gardens. I stood, transfixed by the hedges, flowerbeds, and cobbled paths. An avenue lined with olive-trees, asks us to remember those who fell in the wars, while precious trees, rare and beautiful, lift away those cares. In the centre, a tower stands, Arabesque, pagoda-style, edged with lavic pumicestone, inviting us to study the birds just as Florence Trevelyan intended when she had them built.

Leaving the gardens we set out for the ancient Greektheatre (the *teatroGreco)*. Struck by its magnificence, hard to see it as a ruin (it's still used for operas, plays and concerts).
It was reconstructed by the Romans and used for gladiatorial shows. I wonder: would I have sat here cheering them on, would I have enjoyed the fights, and the savagery. The theatre stands at the top of a hill, and the incline of the valley is designed for seating. Mt. Etna and the Calabrian mountains in the background, offer a stage of natural

beauty. We walk, in awe, up and down, the seats, and back again, standing still, in place, from time to time, imagining, imagining, that time had stood still and we were really here in its heyday …

It's hard to leave Taormina but we move on in great anticipation: Ortigia lies ahead.

Siricusa; Ortigia

The towering *Duomo*, stands in a magnificent setting in the *Piazza del Duomo* , fronting onto a huge open space populated by beautiful people socializing under spectacular chandeliers. The *Duomo* was once the Greek Temple of Athena and had a giant gold statue of the goddess on its roof. The massive Doric columns of the temple are still visible. The wall above the columns along *Via Minerva*, with battlements, is Norman in origin, while the Baroque facade was a replacement after the 1693 earthquake.

Ortigia is not big: 1 km. long and 500 km. wide, so it would be very easy to get around in a day. We decide to walk and explore: first the *Temple of Apollo*, an impressive ruin of the oldest Greek temple, which, being built in the 7th Century BC, was supposedly the first great Doric temple of its kind in Sicily;

Then the *Fonte Aretusa* (on the western shore)

which is a fresh-water spring whose history goes back to the earliest Greek colonists. According to mythology, the spring is an embodiment of the nymph Arethusa, changed into a watercourse by her goddess Artemis/Diana in order to escape the attentions of unwanted suitor Alpheus (Alfeo). Surrounded by high stone walls, planted with papyrus and inhabited by white ducks, the spring is an important place at the water front.

The Catacombs of St. John in Siricusa

The Catacombs of St. John gripped me like nothing before had ever done.

We enter the *Catacombs* through the *Chiesa di San Giovanni*, now a ruin. A beautiful rose window is still visible on the facade. Down in the *Catacombs* we stop at the exact place where *St. Paul* preached; and I feel 2,000 years disappear and I am now in the *anno domini.* We move on through honeycombed tunnels of empty coffins, 20,000 Early Christian tombs that were long ago looted of their "burial riches" by plundering grave robbers.

The Catacombs of St. John gripped me like nothing before had ever done.

Parco Archaeologico

Our first stop was the *Teatro Greco,* the Greek Theatre. The ancient seats have been largely eaten away by time, but you can still stand on the remnants of the stone stage where plays by Euripedes were mounted. I had an eerie sense of time collapsing, of being there to give *Euripedes* a standing ovation.

Outside the entrance to the Greek Theatre we see the most famous of the ancient quarries, *Latomia del Paradiso (Paradise Quarry).* A most unusual cave captures me as I turn a corner in the quarry. The entrance is almost cathedral-like. *Caravaggio* is reputed to have dubbed it the *'Ear of Dionysius'* because of its unusual shape -- it's nearly 60m (197 ft.) long.

Back in Ortigia

We walk back to the *Piazza del Duomo* and enter the *Chiesa di Santa Lucia alla Badia.* The stunning painting of the burial of *St. Lucia* hangs inside. *(St. Lucia is the patron saint of Siricusa/Ortigia.)* *Caravaggio* painted this when he lived in Siricusa, after he escaped from Rome.

Modica

Next stop: *Modica!* The chocolate place!

Modica has a 400 year tradition of Sicilian chocolate-making. The Spanish brought Cacao back from South America and today Modica still specialises in making granulous chocolate, often flavoured with chilli pepper, cinnamon or vanilla, that is based on Aztec methods and recipes.

We see farm country all around and we know the town is divided into two parts: *Alto* and *Basso* ("higher" Modica and "lower" Modica), Houses seem to climb upwards, as though they had been built on top of each other. Churches, with domes, bell towers and facades, rise between the red-tiled roofs. I had no urge to climb those streets. But I wanted my easel and my paints. My camera would never capture *Modica*. We park on *Basso* and walk into town.

A sign on the street notes that Modica's famous sons include the poet Salvadore Quasimodo who won the Nobel Prize in 1959 and Tomaso Campella who cured syphyllis.

In the oldest chocolate shop, *Antica Dolceria Bonajuto* we buy lots of goodies. Then we stop at the *Caffe Macchiato* and relish the most delicious drink : *Caffe Macchiato con scaglie di cioccolata modicana e cannella*: an espresso with cinnamon flavoured chocolate and cream.

Agrigento and The Valley of the Temples

The town is spread over two hills - the hill
of Girgenti, to the west, and the Rupe Atenea,
to the east – and, on an elevated plain sits The
Valley of the Temples. It looks incongruous,
almost like a Disney creation. 'awesome' is
the only adjective that fits. I stand, humbled,
beside those massive doric columns, gazing
over the valley below, imagining the Greeks
(the goddess Persephone), the Romans, the
Normans, the Spanish, the Arabs, the
Carthaginians – all these at various times in
the history.

The Temple of Hercules, one of the most
beautiful , now stands in ruins. Only 9 of its
38 columns stand tall today, and yet, still
visible from far away, it rises, a symbol of
Hercules power and strength

We walk among fallen columns and temples
that lie in ruins like pieces of lego waiting to
be re-connected until we reach the Temple of
Concordia, simple and perfect, standing like
new.Built around 430 B.C., converted in 597
A.D. into a Christian basilica by Bishop
Gregorio, it now stands empty and proud, no
sign of any conversion, erected on an elegant
columnade, 6 by 13, every column, 6.75
metres high. I stand reverently inside, reverent
of the architect and builders that created
this temple, that now moves me.

Marsala

Marsala is internationally famous for one thing: wine. The present-day name is derived from the Arabic "Marsa Allah", meaning "Port of God". We reach the city centre and park in the *Piazza Del Poplo*. Then we walk up the main street and visit the *Duomo*. Afterwards we cross to a café and order marsala wine. Then we go to the Garibaldi Gate, the place where he landed. They do a 'red shirt' commemoration march every year.

We walk back to our car to start the last part of our Sicilian Odyssey. We have reservations at Baglio Oneto near Trapani.

Baglio Oneto

Baglio Oneto is a resort located in Marsala countryside, just a few minutes from Trapani. The Baglio's name comes from the noun "Baal" meaning the interior patio and also from the Latin "Vallum," fortress, stronghold. The Oneto's name derives from the family owners, winemakers. It sits on a hill about 150 meters above sea level, in a place which overlooks a breathtaking landscape.

Our room, off a long tiled corridor, is shuttered and overlooks the pool. We throw open the shutters to view the sunset, but we later regret that because we are invaded by large predatory mosquitoes that plague us all night.

Dining is exclusive, and the patrons are exclusive too! Nevertheless, the service is diligent and the menu extensive.

For our second evening's dining we leave the *Baglio Oneto* and drive a short distance to *Armony Ristorante Pizzeria,* a local restaurant and pizzeria. Set back in its own grounds, it offers plenty of parking space and a huge busy joyous interior. We seem to be the only non-locals. Soon the restaurant is overrun by masses of young people, accompanied by their parents and teachers. The atmosphere is electric.

We have pizza – from a menu with many choices – the best pizza we've ever eaten. A delicious bottle of local wine and lots of personal care and attention make this very special.

And so ended our Sicilian Odyssey, an experience that has remained with me. I'll end this as I began it, in the words of John Ashbery: "To be a writer and write things you must have experiences you can write about. Just living won't do."

AUTOBIOGRAPHY

An autobiography of sorts ...early adventures in the New World

48 dollars and a battered suitcase

An autobiography of sorts ...early adventures in the New World...as a flat stone, splash by splash, skims the surface and escapes the depths, this too will skim the surface and avoid the depths.

Treading Water

At nineteen I left Ireland for the first time. The ferry across the Irish Sea from Belfast to Stranraer was overcrowded and uncivil. Families huddled together, to keep warm, on the cold decks. Young men got drunk as the long night passed. In the inside lounge, cigarette smoke hung in a haze like a London fog. The train that rattled me through the sleeping heart of England at night was no better. Cold hard seats and indifferent stares from my fellow passengers reinforced my isolation, my sense of desolation. Every part of my body ached when I disembarked from British Rail at Euston Station on a steely cold Sunday morning. I made my way into the city and sat in Trafalgar Square, overawed at the imperial weight of the Empire all around me. Days later, after the first shock of seeing *'No Irish or Coloured'* on the three by four cards advertising flat and bedsit vacancies, I eventually found a place to stay. The landlady

was a kind woman who felt sorry for me in
the same way that she would have felt sorry
for a stray cat.

Splash One

Two years later I left England and emigrated
to Canada. I sailed from Liverpool on the
Empress of England, a 28 thousand ton
Canadian Pacific ship. I felt that I was
following in the footsteps of the pilgrims,
setting out by ship for the New World…in
mid-Atlantic I watched the curve of the earth
on the horizon, confirming that I was sailing
on the surface of this wondrous planet, our
Earth. It was humid when I disembarked in
Quebec. I climbed the 350 steps to the Plains
of Abraham at 2 am, wondering what it had
been like when the Irish General Wolfe met
the French General Montcalm on that
battlefield, each fighting to win a stake in the
New World, and I was fighting to stay the
course as I climbed those steps, higher and
higher…later (much later) I had my very first
'hamburger with the works' in a bar in
Quebec City that could just as easily have
been in Marseilles.   We boarded again and
disembarked for the last time in Montreal,
tagged for entry with an immigrant label
attached to my lapel, I boarded the train for
Toronto, (arriving with $48 dollars and a
battered suitcase) to find myself sitting alone
in an office filled with other immigrants.

Splash Two

I ended up in lodgings in Toronto where the landlady took $18 dollars from me before she'd permit me to follow her to the top floor where I found my new home, a simple metal bed and a threadbare mattress. There were no jobs in Toronto, weeks earlier people had lined up for soup, but I must have been impervious to all that …

Splash Three

I tried to find work anywhere and everywhere and I even applied to join the Royal Canadian Mounted Police – to find out weeks later that I had passed the written tests but failed the physical (too skinny). With my money running out and no-one to fall back on I finally found a job at the T. Eaton Company department store, selling yard goods (material by the yard) and 'notions' (i.e. buttons, fasteners, hooks, etc). But first, a day's orientation where I learned that young Timothy Eaton had emigrated from County Antrim in Ireland and had founded the company from his first store on Yonge Street …and it gave me a shot of that North American confidence that would build stronger and stronger in me over time. I still remember my most famous customer: *Celia Franca,* founder and director of the National Ballet of Canada, who would sweep into my department with a grand dramatic flourish, seeking outfits for her next ballet

Splash Four

In the evening I attempted to sell Colliers encyclopedias door to door in unsuspecting villages north of Toronto. Launched on this escapade on the very first night by a tall charismatic black American, I was assigned to work with a Dutchman, a pro at this work. He would join in and kick ball with kids out playing on a street and learn their names and where they lived, enough knowledge to let us gain entry to homes that might be good prospects. But it had its danger: when the man of one house shut the door in my face and then sent his huge Alsatian dog after me, leaving me barely enough time to close the metal gate that sealed the high fence that surrounded the property.

Splash Five

Finally the day arrived to leave Canada for the USA. I had saved the princely sum of $400. The guard on the train from Toronto to New York checked my immigration documents and asked me for my address in the USA. Somewhat taken aback when he discovered that I did not have one, he admonished me and said ' *you'd better notify the State Department of your address within three weeks'* And that's the unvarnished description of my entry into the USA, heading for New York with nowhere to stay and no job waiting for me.

Splash Six

'Holed up' in a fifth floor walk-up apartment in a Bronx tenement building, sharing with five other Irish immigrants, I squeezed into the IRT subway every morning to start my day as a filing clerk at a major bank. Five months later, barely acclimatized to the USA, I received a *'greetings from Uncle Sam'* letter, directing me to report for induction into the US Army. So I had to choose: leave the country or serve two years in the army. I had no intention of leaving so I had only one choice: report for induction and basic training at Fort Dix, New Jersey.

Splash Seven

I started eight weeks of rigorous basic training at Fort Dix. Nothing had prepared me for this experience. Physically and mentally arduous, it de-constructed and re-constructed me, converting me into a disciplined, fit, and capable soldier. I survived the daily drills, the long marches carrying a full field pack, metal helmet, gas mask, and my M14 rifle with bayonet, the planes dropping tear gas from the air on us. Then the hand-to-hand combat and weapons training: target shooting, and night firing with infra-red sights. The infiltration course simulated battlefield conditions - executed in daytime and again at night; we threw hand grenades, then crawled eighty yards, with our weapons, passed sand-bagged bunkers that exploded, crawled under barbed wire as red tracer bullets flew overhead. And finally winning my sharpshooter medal for expertise with the M14 rifle was my prized achievement.

Splash Eight

After basic training I was shipped to Fort Sam Houston, Texas, to be trained as a medic. At Fort Sam they trained me in everything: giving injections, suturing wounds, taking x-rays, applying pressure bandages over chest/lung injuries, giving mouth-to-mouth resuscitation, giving enemas, how to treat a patient in shock, how to do a tracheotomy, how to splint a broken limb ... But I still found time to enjoy San Antonio. One strong memory is the day I visited the Alamo, a place that always seemed to be in my consciousness. I was amazed to discover how many of my fellow countrymen from Ireland died there; I could even claim Davy Crockett because his grandfather and father were born in Ireland (although some say his father was born on the ship on the way over).

Splash Nine

Assigned to Korea, I left San Antonio for Oakland, Calfornia. From there I flew to Ancorage, Alaska, and eventually on to Kishine Barracks in Yokohama, Japan: (and I borrow the memory from an earlier poem) *Once, long ago, I landed at Tachikawa and drove madly through the night to Yokohama. But that's only a memory. So long ago, sometimes it seems that I've imagined it, until now*   Kishine was the stepping off point (or I should say, the 'lifting off') for Korea. When that day arrived we were loaded onto a large transport plane, seated on webbing attached to the inside fuselage where we could see the cavernous belly of the plane below us. Armed with box lunches, we set off. This journey ended with my arrival at the 43rd MASH, near Uijongbu (the same MASH that inspired the book and the TV series) where I would spend the next thirteen months (much 'deep water' treaded in these thirteen months but I won't go deeper here).

Splash Ten

Thirteen months later I returned to the US to serve my remaining five months at Fort Knox, Kentucky, before being discharged …

And so commences my romance with America and my pursuit of the American Dream. But these are 'deep, deep waters' and I need to be properly attired before diving in. This small volume, KNOWING, is much too shallow for that. Perhaps, on some future day, I will don wet suit and oxygen tank, and dive in.

Pat Mullan

Pat Mullan is a thriller writer, poet, and artist. He was born in Ireland and has lived in England, Canada and the USA. He now lives in Connemara, in the west of Ireland.

You can visit him at: **www.patmullan.com**

Other works by Pat Mullan:

THRILLERS

The Circle of Sodom:
http://amzn.to/15WQNgQ

Blood Red Square
http://amzn.to/189ZWBS

Last Days of The Tiger
http://amzn.to/16I2DJi

Creatures of Habit
http://amzn.to/WBCqFK

POETRY

Childhood Hills:
http://amzn.to/1000L9P

Awakening
http://amzn.to/10pyEji

James Dickey's Poetry:
The Religious Dimension
http://amzn.to/YjnaDM

SHORT WORK

Galway Girl
http://amzn.to/X2lkDa

Tribunal
http://amzn.to/10022xq

Screwed
http://amzn.to/11SRzY2

The Avenger
http://amzn.to/156S05x

Facsimile
http://amzn.to/156SgBN

Galway Noir
http://bit.ly/ZTy8OK

Eleven Days in July
http://amzn.to/12X499z

www.ingramcontent.com/pod-product-compliance
Lightning Source LLC
Chambersburg PA
CBHW031329040426
42443CB00005B/262

*9 7 8 0 9 8 3 8 6 5 2 1 6 *